To Publish Or Not To Publish...

...And How!

by Sandra Adams

ISBN: 978-1512080728
First Edition 2015

Forward

Self publishing today is hardly *ever* true self-publishing. My husband Gary and I have run the gamut of every possible method of publishing a book, from a brick and mortar publishing house to those "assisted publishing" sites – more than one – to simply formatting and sending to a printer, and finally, the ultimate in self-publishing – the DIY with help method. So many people have picked what is left of my brain about which ones work best, why we chose what we chose at different times, and ultimately, if I can help them to publish their work. The answer is yes, I could. That is not, however the message of this little book. The message needs to be two-fold: what is your goal, and what are your skills? Think about those two questions as you begin to read the following missive about how you can tell your story – when you believe you have a story to tell!

Table Of Contents

Chapter One
Intro To Publishing

The digital age has swept up just about every industry in the world, from communications to manufacturing. Publishing, however, for some reason, has fallen behind. It seems astonishing to some that we still offer physical books, when ebooks and books on tape are so much more available, inexpensive and, frankly, easier to "read."

Many of us who grew up in the non-digital age are content to hold a physical book in our hands, yet on occasion, such as traveling to another country, appreciate the convenience of a e-reader of some sort. Still, some stories simply demand something to put in the hands of the reader, and to that historical end, being able to publish and print your story in a cost-effective way is getting easier.

What has gotten more challenging though is figuring out the very best method for you personally. One needs to be able to assess their own skill set in terms of word processing, formatting, uploading, designing, and marketing a book. I for one took a long time to get up to speed on most of it, struggling with such things as "margins" and "gutter" and "bleed." If you have absolutely not the vaguest notion what these things are, you are in good company. Luckily, in almost every avenue of publishing now, if you can *read,* you can handle these things without completely understanding why they work the way they work.

I won't bother to explain all of those terms to you. If you are so inclined to learn about them, dear reader, you are on your own. The questions that have come my way are uncomplicated, but the answers vary, depending on the competence of the questioner, and so it is up to you to divine how these answers will apply to you.

There really is no one to ask simple questions and get simple answers, because everyone has a vested interest in passing out education and information – including me! Most people are disinclined to work for free, at least to any great degree. Answering questions, though, is not exactly considered work, until it requires much time away from one's own work. In that vein, I hope to provide, at a pamphlet price, answers to the most commonly asked questions about publishing in the 21st century.

In the interest of not putting myself in a position of legal trouble, I will not use the names of any of the companies we have used with one distinct exception – Create Space – the publishing platform of this book! You will read much more about this avenue in another chapter. For now, I hope to make this book somewhat interactive. At the end of each chapter, you will have space to write down any questions you have, and when you finish the book, you should feel free to email and ask your questions.

You should also know that there are now many professionals available to assist with just about any stage of production. Just be prepared to pay a fee. Each person has their own "glitches" in skill set, and mine was the formatting glitch. Finally, several solutions have been presented that are both suitable and cost effective.

Each author has to decide what price tag they place on telling their story. If you decide that your story is worth either the time investment and/or the financial investment, then you should be able to wend your way through the options available to you with the information from this book.

Next step – publishing options!

QUESTIONS?

_____

_____

_____

_____

_____

_____

_____

_____

_____

_____

Chapter Two
Brick And Mortar

This is the most traditional – and the most difficult – avenue to choose. Why? Because almost no agent will bother to read an unsolicited manuscript, and thus, generally are only interested in works by known authors. Most agents are looking for authors who have already published..... something successful. Makes for a perfect opportunity for "sheep stealing" between agents, such as one would find in pro sports.

If an author is fortunate enough to find a decent agent to take them on as a client, the next tremendous step is for them to be able to get your work in front of a publisher with an iota of interest – again – in an unproven author.

How did Danielle Steel get to be top selling author? I have no idea, but I do know that the most prolific authors seem to lose the special quality of their writing as they produce book after book after book. I am told that many contracts lock these authors in to agreements that demand a given number of works in a given length of time. Simply put, produce or you are finished. I don't know about you, but I write from the heart, from life, and to a need and hopefully, a market. I can't imagine writing simply to regurgitate a story for a publisher to market under contract.

Of course, the income generated from the ongoing bilge of words that escape into the public each year seems attractive; but how much better to be known for quality works in your especial niche! Sure, you say!

Here is a brief breakdown on the cons and pros of agreements most common to this type of publishing:

THE CONS

1. control and rights to the work almost always remain with the publisher for the duration of the contract – or life
2. availability of sales and marketing information are almost always out of reach for the author
3. cost of production generally will limit the author's ability to purchase sufficient numbers of books for resale, and those resales might even be contractually limited
4. some level of creative decision-making – such as the title – can be usurped by the publisher
5. some publishers will require all control over all aspects of production, from other forms of reading material to on-screen production, such as turning your children's' story into a movie.
6. royalties are not paid monthly in most cases, and if you are awarded an advance, you can often wait for years to see another dime.

7. marketing choices, promotions and other methods of getting your book publicity are most often controlled strictly by the publisher.
8. publishers may well demand that any future works by an author be awarded to that publisher
9. sales channels are most often chosen by the publishers, and outside sales can be restricted
10. price is set by the publisher, and so would be the royalties.

THE PROS
1. you don't have to do any of the formatting work
2. you don't typically have to do the marketing
3. you may get some help in acquiring the rights to photos needed for your book – maybe
4. easier to produce a hard cover to often available through many self-publishing firms

5. many will make books available for signings and other events at no cost to the author
6. more expanded channels for sales

Between the pros and the cons, I would expect that an author-hopeful will have to find something in between the brick and mortar avenue and the several other choices, unless of course one has a relative to whom they are speaking within the publishing industry. Creative control can end up being a deal breaker, as can contractual restraints on either party, usually the author. It is important to read and re-read any contract, and preferably have an attorney examine it for holes, control issues, and in the end, a bad deal for the author. After all, it is your story to tell, isn't it?

QUESTIONS?

_____

_____

_____

_____

_____

_____

_____

_____

_____

_____

_____

Chapter Three
"Self-Publishing" Online Firms

We have published multiple books through two different companies, and there are real pluses to doing it this way, especially if you have not the faintest desire to be involved in the production of the book. You should be well aware of both the reputations of these companies and the widely varying prices of them. One firm may charge a production fee of perhaps $900 for your 50 pages color-illustrated children's book, but each copy would cost you $12.50 to purchase for resale, with a ten copy minimum. It is a great way to fill your extra bedroom with a few hundred books that may take two years to sell!

In addition, some packages on different sites also have wide price differentials. In addition, while one firm might charge $20 for each additional *page* with changes after initial submission, others will want $20 *per line* with a change. It can really add up if you do not read those contracts carefully. Also, paying attention to what is included in each package at each firm is mind numbing, and so it became clear to us that we needed a method to our initial madness.

This was my job, and I will share with you how I managed to sort out the many choices. At each website, I printed a page or two that compared their packages available. I then compared those choices between each firm. Some were eliminated quickly due to their high package prices. Others needed comparisons on itms such as formatting fees, purchasing costs, and even marketing materials. Yes, most provide a few little materials to help the author market their own book. After all, it is in the firm's interest as well to have the books marketed.

From one firm, we got a full box of marketing materials, such as book marks, postcards, event mailers, 11" x 16" laminated flyers, and the like. Unfortunately, the next book, published with a different firm – and cost twice as much – only included some poorly printed (what a shocker *that* was!)letter-sized flyers, a few dozen small postcards, and a promotional letter, for what I am sure I don't know. Clearly, an author can think up their own words!

We eventually went back to the first firm to publish our third book, and were pleased with the production. I would add that if you do not have the money to go this route either, it is time to get up to speed on your own publishing skills! Still, it was a relief, especially early in our publishing career, to be able to rely on paid professionals to do those tough jobs. We have been pleased with the product in every case. The lowdown?

CONS

1. still some formatting and uploading of files to be done
2. the fees are variable but still a consideration, from $900 to upwards of $5000 for publishing packages
3. extras vary as widely as the prices do, and price is not an indicator of what an author will get either in services or extras
4. it is a jungle, navigating through all of the possibilities
5. wholesale pricing is about the same as the dedicated publishing house pricing, so no real savings there
6. no control over sales channels
7. no advance payments

PROS

1. more control over content and creativity
2. more control over pricing
3. better options for style and size
4. much more limited contractual limitations

5. product quality is excellent
6. did I mention that the author has more control?

Between the pros and cons, we would still opt for this avenue rather than fight the not-so-good fight of acquiring an agent and then a publisher. A creative person capable of producing a marketable work is also capable of making many of the decisions themselves, and one of those decisions can open the door to being 'discovered" by a really big and more successful publisher who can market on a word-wide scale

Also, to my knowledge, most of these self-publishing firms do offer their clients' books on amazon, B & N and other top channels. That in itself is a great bargain!

QUESTIONS?

_____

_____

_____

_____

_____

_____

_____

_____

_____

_____

_____

Chapter Four
Just The Printing, Ma'am

We wanted to try something new and different – and cheaper – and so decided to try doing all the work ourselves, and then sending it to a printer who we knew. In this way, we knew that we would have total control of everything – but – we also would have to do everything, from acquiring the ISBN number to formatting... everything. It was with considerable trepidation that we – I – entered into this jungle. It was exhausting, and in the end, I did have to ask for help. For a minimal fee, and I mean minimal, the in-house formatting specialist was able to format the jumble of content that I had sent on a thumb drive.

I would add that for any and all of the methods described herein, any and all illustrations or photos must be of a minimum dpi quality, but also be of legal usage – in other words, *no one* wants to get sued for illegally using a photo. It would then be your job to get permissions from anything you chose to use that you do not own the rights to.

Having worked in both banking and for an accountant, I considered myself to be fairly well-organized, but this particular avenue was one of the most frustrating and challenging things I have ever undertaken, on par with writing a symphony alone. As I said, eventually I enlisted – and paid for – the services of the in-house formatter, and was relieved when he responded with affirmation of success. There is nothing more humbling than having to ask for help doing something that you believed, in error, that you were perfectly trained to do. It was worth it, however, and I highly recommend shedding any pride you might have about the technical part, so that the creative part can shine!

With most forms of publishing, even with a dedicated publishing house, make sure that you have available a decent editor, both for content and formatting. You yourself must be willing to critically edit your own work. One of my pet peeves is "spell Check." Why? Because it will never correct "form" when what I *meant* to type was "from." An aspiring author also needs to be willing to hear criticism, and in fact, be willing to make changes in order to make the work better. You can tell your story, but you had better be willing to work with an editor.

If you have no one else available, it is advisable to at *least* procure the services of a quality editor, since the trouble of telling your story ought to at least be approved by one the person before you bother sent it to the public. I am fortunate – my husband has been writing for forty years, and has several books published. We edit each others' books, and doing so has been a real growing lesson in listening to one another. I would say that probably publishing together can really strengthen a marriage, or possibly blow it sky-high, if one or the other has major pride issues. Get over it.

With what I call the "Go To Print" method, none of these services is offered, and so you will need to find and pay for them somewhere else.

Secondarily, format editing is an artistic skill, and what seems to look just fine in Word can be a real mess once uploaded and converted to accommodate those gutters, margins and bleeds. You should find someone who will do this for you. With the advent of true self publishing, the other firms are trying to hang on to their market share, much as the brick and mortar are trying to hold on to theirs.

You will also need to be able to do the set up to offer your book in eBook form, because a print house will not be doing any of that, we found out. For us, eBooks were a secondary thought, partly because we were already struggling with the print forms, and also because we simply wanted to first make sure people could hold a real book in their hands. we wanted to hold it in ours!

The quality is somewhat less, and I think understandably so, because these print companies are mainly designed to print flyers and posters and such, not books. Binding become an issue, as does color interiors, due to the high cost of offset printing. Print On Demand – a staple of other forms of publishing, especially trade paperbacks – is not available from this method of publishing. An author would need to be prepared to order a few hundred at a time to make it worth the cost and the printer's time. Still, if an author is completely competent in the way of formatting the entire project, this may be the most cost-effective way to go, while retaining all rights and controls. I would say though that it was really tough going. I don't recommend it

CONS
1. author must know how to do everything or pay someone else
2. a little bit lower binding quality
3. author must acquire ISBN number
4. all marketing and promotion is done by author
5. no extras
6. costly wholesale purchases
7. no free authors copy

PROS
1. COMPLETE control
2. all creative rights
3. all marketing control
4. can be cheaper per unit

For someone who is quite brilliant in this kind of processing, this is probably the most cost-effective way to go. Since I am not that proficient, it os not my first choice. Keep in mind that, as in most cases, the author will be responsible for all rights to photos etc. There will be no one there to shepherd you into the correct way to protect yourself, and they will not be liable. Still, it is an adventure!

QUESTIONS?

_____

_____

_____

_____

_____

_____

_____

_____

_____

_____

_____

_____

_____

COOKERY SHMOOKERY

16 Easy-Makin', Great-Tastin' Recipes

Sandra Adams

Chapter Five
The Rest of the Story

After publishing one book with a dedicated publisher, three with self-publishing firms online, and one book by way of a private printer, we finally opted for a solution that could ultimately blend my slowly-acquired skills in formatting and a level of creative talent – mainly for the cover design. This venue had not been available even a year earlier, and its predecessor had still required far too much understanding of gutters, etc. I steadfastly refused to learn about any of that stuff!

Finally, I stumbled upon a new method of publishing that at this point has taken the self-publishing world by absolute storm – Create Space. In 2013, I was able to successfully produce and publish and market two books, "Camptown Races" and "Endurance Log".

Creature Comforts

When Your Pet Says
Goodbye...And Other Things

Sandra Adams

An Amazon company, the opportunity for marketing was clear, and the system was exciting! As I am typing now, I know that, from the moment my script is approved by my "editor", I will be able to upload, format, and design a cover within about a day. There is no fee at all to do this, but of course, you will need to have your files all upload ready in an acceptable form.

For example, any and all illustrations and photos must be a minimum dpi of 300, and the content formatting must be pdf or Word.doc. If there is a problem with any part of your script or images, the system will kick them back to you with a message about what needs to be corrected. Lovely!

The system does take a while to learn, but it is considerably simpler than any other! Depending on your creative genius, you will be able to either use their trouble-free method of building your book, or strike out on your own, with open templates available to upload your own cover or choose a different text or spacing style. I would add that it is just as important to have your work edited thoroughly, because, aside from spelling and a few sentence structure and character issues, the system is not designed to correct for poor grammar or incomplete sentences.

CONS

1. you will have to do the work yourself
2. time-consuming the first few times
3. so far not set up for producing hard covers in the system
4. limited to self-marketing and sales and/or Amazon, unless you buy a separate ISBN

PROS

1. superbly easy to produce once learned
2. considerably less expensive than other methods
3. fairly fast to ship
4. no minimum for you purchases for resale
5. ability to ship qualities to buyers directly from CS, saving shipping expenses
6. author sets price, and thus, royalties
7. world-wide distribution
8. almost unlimited options to create the look you want

9. additional assistance is available for a fee, but most will likely not need it
10. no fear of having your manuscript rejected
11. easy-access assistance if you have a question or problem

Once you have completed all of the steps, generally your book will go live within about a day, and you will be able to find it on Amazon. When you find it, you will be able to click on the Facebook logo and share your new book! Also, Amazon keeps a monitor of sales rankings for you.

What are the steps working with this system? Choosing a title and selecting other information, such as illustrator, other contributors, etc. Create Space will assign a free ISBN number that applies only to Amazon sales. You must purchase another number if you wish to market through other channels, such as Barnes & Noble.

Next, you will be asked to select genre, subtitle, if any, and book size. You will have a choice between matte and glossy exterior, paper color, and whether or not to use color or black and white interior. You should know that choosing a color interior adds a fairly significant amount to the price and cost of the book. It is certainly doable, and *you* don't pay anything out, but you do want your book to be priced to sell easily. A really great book with stunning color photos won't matter if no one buys it because it costs $32.

Next, you will be asked to upload your interior file, and that is where you must be prepared. I will explain to you what I have found to be the most useful way to do this in the next section. For now, let's assume you have uploaded your interior, including interior "matter" – that is, ISBN number, forward or dedication, Table of Contents, etc.

Once you have uploaded it, you will be informed that it has been submitted for review. Once you and Create Space have reviewed it, you will be notified of any formatting issues. This may take a day or so, an in the meantime, there are other things to do!

In the meantime, you can go to the Cover Creator and create or upload a great cover. The directions are pretty clear, and the process is easy. That also will be uploaded and submitted for review. It will take a day or so for this to go through the review process. You will also receive a digital proof online so that you can check out your uploads, while CS continues to review. You will also be invited to set a price, royalty level and to select sales channels. There are other and sundry "house cleaning" items to tie up while you wait, and by the time you do these things, you should be able to set the project aside for the night and wait for morning, when you are certain to have a review response.

Now that you have an idea about the process, let me share with you what *not* to do. Sometimes the best lessons are the ones learned the hard way, but I would love to save you the trouble of converting files so many times and doing so much formatting that you first lose track of which file is the most up to date, and secondly, lose your hair. The templates require that your files be uploaded in a format that is acceptable to the system. There are plenty of assists available on the system to help you set margins and such on your own word processing program, but in general, simply using page set-up will work. It is for me a three-step process.

First, I complete and edit the manuscript on standard letter sized page set-up. After fully editing and approving the file, I will create a second document in the size that matches the book trim size I have chosen. To make sure I have a file that will not need further formatting, I do go into the program and double check the margins needed. Once this is confirmed, the new file (a 6" x 9" for example) will now be formatted on the word processor, and this is where I will insert other interior material and information, such as the table of contents. Also, if you have illustrations of any kind, this is the time to insert them, making sure that they also sit between the proper margins limits. It is assumed here that you have already resized your illustrations so that they are at least 300 dpi, and are already cropped to your taste.

It is advisable to save your work periodically, so that if your computer throws a tantrum, or shuts down, you will not lose your work. Once you have inserted your illustrations and fully double and triple checked your material, you are ready to upload to the system. Be sure to upload this particular file, and remember, if you are creating your file as something other than a pdf or doc file, you will need to first convert it.

One particular feature that I very much love is that you are able at any time to go into the system and change or update your work! Yes! If you find errors, you are able to make those changes to the file you uploaded , make your changes, and upload it again. Should you choose to swap out a photo, you may do that, too. If you decide you prefer matte to glossy finish, go right in and change it up! You can even change the entire cover! The message here is that YOU are in control! Got it now? By the way, if you find typos in this book, please let me know – I am used to criticism, ad the fixes are easy!

QUESTIONS?

_____

_____

_____

_____

_____

_____

_____

Chapter Six
Last Words of Instruction

As you embark on this most intriguing of journeys, there are a few cautions for you. Again, having learned a few of these the hard way, I would like to save you from yourselves, as I wish someone hd saved me from myself a few times.

It has come to me that for a book such as this, more informational in nature, the 5" x 8" trim size is more suitable. Both of my Equestrian Logs are of this size, and fit perfectly into saddle packs, glove boxes, and even some back pockets. For most fiction and non-fiction stories, the standard 6" x 9" trade paperbacks is most common and most popular. We have produced both ourselves, and for books that are mainly text, this is a good choice. For books that are heavy with illustrations, other options are available, including a portrait formatted 8" x 11", and a 8.5" x 8.5". Choose wisely!

Secondly, write the very best manuscript you possibly can, then edit it, read it, have someone else edit it, re-read it, and the go with it. If you can find

a local writer's club, join up! Learn to take criticism well, and don't be afraid to make recommended changes if you think that they have value.

Thirdly, put together a good introduction letter for your book, something suitable for marketing your book to local, private stores and the like. Also, plan a few events ahead whether it is a private signing with friends and family, or buying a space at a local Bazaar. Make sure you have a copy of the book yourself before ordering, so that you are familiar with your product, and to make sure you didn't miss something that needs attention.

Finally, prepare a marketing plan. This varies as widely as the book subjects in publishing. What works for our books, may not work for yours, but you will need to identify your target audience, buy marketing materials from a site such as Vista Print, and don't forget to map out an attractive display table. Use Twitter, Pinterist and

Facebook to your advantage and consider building a website to offer your books more widely than on Amazon. I should add here that Amazon provides many book keeping pluses, from tax forms for year end reporting to monthly totals and sales records. Utilize these! They will be your best friend in April.

Don't be put off when someone tells you that your manuscript needs this or that. Consider it a compliment that they were interested in editing it in the first place! At least you won't have to deal with being rejected by Random House! Remember, if someone you ask to read your manuscript refuses, it may be that they have trouble giving feedback, because sometime spell don't want to criticize. Take it in stride – and find someone else to read it.

Part of the reason for publishing this was to provide answers to some questions that I get asked so often these days that some days I feel like I am talking to myself. Providing this information in this way also gives the reader a chance to hold in their own hands the product of what we would consider the every best way to publish, at least from our several years of experience now. What you are holding in your hands it the product of Create Space, and I would do it again… and again… and again. In fact, I am!

For your questions that you most certainly noted as you read, please feel free to email me at drquinndsa@mac.com to ask those questions. You may also visit our website at www.garyadamsbooks.com to see who our very first foray into website construction produced. As you move forward with your project, you may have more questions. Just make notes and ask! Above all, keep writing! Keep on writing! We all have a story to tell!

So Flat,
So Deep,
So Far

Books offered by
www.garyadamsbooks.com

How The Little Clock Lost His Hands
The Little Clock Who Had No Hands
The Litte Clock Who Had Two Hands

So Flat, So Deep, So Far
The Ladybug Story
Conversations with Coach Wooden: On Baseball, Heroes and Life

Camptown Races
Endurance Log
For The Sport Of It Log
Creature Comforts: When Your Pet Says Goodbye… And Other Things
Cookery Shmookery

Coming Soon
The Gentleman Stallion
Four Ordinary Days
The Tiny Fish